J

3|93

GREAT BATTLES AND SIEGES

THE TROJAN WAR

ELIZABETH EDMONDSON

ILLUSTRATIONS BY
HARRY CLOW

new
Discovery
B·O·O·K·S
New York

Maxwell Macmillan Canada
Toronto

Maxwell Macmillan International
New York • Oxford • Singapore • Sydney

GREAT BATTLES

First American publication 1992 by New Discovery Books, Macmillan Publishing Company, 866 Third Avenue, New York, NY 10022
Maxwell Macmillan Canada Inc., 1200 Eglinton Avenue East, Suite 200, Don Mills, Ontario M3C 3N1

Macmillan Publishing Company is part of the Maxwell Communication Group of Companies

First published in 1992
in Great Britain by
Wayland (Publishers) Ltd
61 Western Road, Hove
East Sussex BN3 1JD
England
First published in Australia by
The Macmillan Company of Australia Pty Ltd
107 Moray Street, South Melbourne
Victoria 3205, Australia

A ZOË BOOK

Devised and produced by
Zoe Books Limited
15 Worthy Lane
Winchester
Hampshire SO23 7AB
England

Printed in Belgium
Design: Pardoe Blacker
Picture research: Sarah Staples
Illustrations: Harry Clow

10 9 8 7 6 5 4 3 2 1

Library of Congress Cataloging-in-Publication Data
Edmondson, Elizabeth.
  The Trojan War/Elizabeth Edmondson.
    p. cm. — (Great battles and sieges)
  Includes bibliographical references and index.
  Summary: Describes the causes, events, and aftermath of the ten-year war between the Trojans and the Greeks.
  ISBN 0-02-733273-X
    1. Trojan War — Juvenile literature. 2. Troy (Extinct city —
Juvenile literature. [1. Trojan War. 2. Troy (Extinct city)
3. Mythology, Greek.] I. Title. II. Series.
  DF221.T8E33   1992
  939'.21 — dc20   91-31860

Photographic acknowledgments

The publishers wish to acknowledge, with thanks, the following photographic sources:

C M Dixon 27, 29; Michael Holford 4b, 13, 24; Kunsthistorisches Museum, Vienna 26; J V Luce 4t; Ronald Sheridan, Ancient Art & Architecture Collection 5t, 6, 7, 9, 12l, 12r, 14, 17l, 18, 22

THE TROJAN WAR

Contents

Fact or Fiction?

On a windswept ridge called Hissarlik, above a plain in western Turkey, lie some of the world's most famous remains. It is hard to tell from the broken-down walls and piles of rubble that this is the place where armies clashed and heroes fought to the death over three thousand years ago. Yet many experts believe that this is the site of the city of Troy.

▶ *The hill of Hissarlik today. The remains of nine cities, one on top of the other, have been discovered here. One of the cities may be the city that Homer called Troy.*

▼ *The poet Homer, whose poems tell the story of Troy. We know very little about Homer. He may have come from the Greek island of Chios, and tradition says that he was blind. Some scholars now think that he may never have existed. They think that the name "Homer" is simply a name for a group of writings or writers.*

Where Was Troy?

The story of the wars between the people of Greece and the people of Troy has been told for more than twenty-five hundred years. It was first told by a Greek poet named Homer in *The Iliad* and *The Odyssey*. Homer composed his poems about five hundred years after the siege of Troy was supposed to have taken place. Because Homer was not there at the time and because the story is such a strange mixture of gods and goddesses, heroes and heroines, people thought that it was just a **legend**. Then, about one hundred years ago, people began to search for the place where Troy may have been. They read Homer's poems very carefully, and they read what other **scholars** had written about Troy. Other people traveled to Hissarlik and drew maps of the area. Then in 1870, a German named Heinrich Schliemann said he had discovered the remains of Troy at Hissarlik. Some experts now believe Homer's poems may be based on a real war that occurred around 1250 B.C, but they have not been able to prove that the ruins at Hissarlik are the remains of Troy.

THE TROJAN WAR

Was There a Trojan War?

Did the Trojan War ever happen? Some people believe that it did, but other people still say that it is just a story, or legend. Homer's poems tell of heroes and heroines who lived and fought in a golden age. Often, stories like these were told or sung by storytellers and bards (poet-singers) long before they were written down. This was the way in which all stories and legends were passed on when only a few people knew how to read and write.

◄ *Heinrich Schliemann (left) had a strange gift for discovering things. Schliemann's digging was very rough: He just went straight down! However, he found walls and the traces of a lost city. Then an archaeologist named Dörpfeld excavated more carefully. He discovered that at Hissarlik there were several buried cities, and at least one of the cities had been destroyed by fire. The date of that city, about 1250 B.C., was right for Homer's Trojan War.*

The Story through the Ages

When people finally wrote down the story of the Trojan War, it was already well-known. The Greeks and Romans all knew the story of Troy, and they nearly all thought that it was true. The story was never forgotten, although for hundreds of years after the time of the Romans few people knew anything about the Greeks or Greek poetry. Then, about five hundred years ago, people began to be interested in Greek and Roman literature. They read Homer's poems and the story came to life again. It has been translated into many languages. We do not need to understand Greek to read the story, but it helps if we understand something about the lives of the people who lived in Greece and Troy three thousand years ago.

▼ *The Mycenaeans lived in small, independent kingdoms in the area now called Greece. They shared a way of life, a language, and religious beliefs, but each kingdom was separate from the others in its government.*

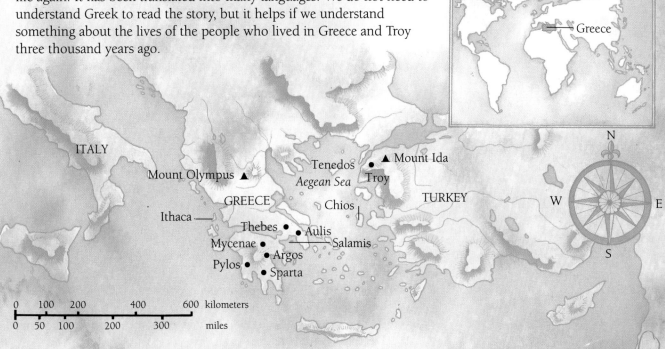

The Mycenaeans

*▶ The ruins of the **citadel** of Mycenae can still be seen today, surrounded by thick stone walls. The ruined royal palace is the building at the top of the hill.*

The army that attacked Troy came from the country we know as Greece, but the soldiers were not Greeks, they were Mycenaeans. This civilization is named after the greatest city of that time, Mycenae. The ruins of the city of Mycenae still stand. Like other city-palaces at that period, Mycenae was strongly fortified. It had thick stone walls and a secret water supply in case of attack. Inside cities such as Mycenae there would have been a palace for the royal family and houses for the members of the royal court. The army headquarters were also inside the city, as well as houses for the soldiers. Skilled craft workers lived there, too. All the offices needed to govern the area were inside the city, as well as places to store grain and other belongings.

Religion

Although we have no detailed information about Mycenaean religion, we can learn a lot by looking at the evidence in wall paintings, called frescoes, and at statues. Goddesses seem to have been more important than gods. They are shown more often, and when a god is shown he is smaller and less important.

The Mycenaeans did not build temples to their gods and goddesses. Instead, they used special rooms inside their palaces or houses for worship. In the Mycenaean society women were priestesses. They made offerings, or **sacrifices**, to the goddesses.

We also know that the Mycenaeans believed in a life after death because, like the people of Egypt, they put belongings into tombs. They thought that these goods would be useful to the person who had died.

THE TROJAN WAR

◀ *The city walls of Troy today. Homer describes Troy as having big walls and high gateways with tight-fitting doors. He speaks of palaces and wide streets.*

Warrior-kings

The Mycenaeans were ruled by chiefs, or kings. Chiefs often went on raiding parties, **plundering** other cities, such as Troy, for their wealth. Weapons and armor found in graves show that the kings were also warriors. Some people think that a raiding party — and not the exciting events described in Homer's stories — may have been the cause of the Trojan War. Other experts think that bad harvests may have caused the Mycenaean kings to become rivals in the attempt to feed their people and that this caused a war.

Troy

Troy was built to withstand a siege, but it was also a city where people lived and worked. In peacetime, boats came and went from the small harbor near the city. The plain around the city provided good grazing for sheep and horses; Troy was famous for its horse breeding.

Inside the citadel, all roads led to the summit of a hill where the royal palace stood. The palace had armories, storerooms, workshops, and bakeries as well as grand rooms for the king and court. It also had a place, called a **shrine,** for worshiping the gods and goddesses.

c. 2000 B.C. Earliest evidence of the Mycenaeans in Greece.

c. 1600 B.C. Mycenaean civilization at the height of its power.

c. 1250 B.C. Traditional date of the fall of Troy.

c. 1200 B.C. Beginning of the decline of the Mycenaean civilization.

GREAT BATTLES

The Players

Homer's story of the Trojan War is full of heroes and heroines, gods and goddesses. The heroes in the story are often in danger of dying or being killed. They can die, so they are called **mortals**. The gods and goddesses cannot die — they are **immortals**. The gods play tricks on one another as well as on the heroes and heroines, and they quarrel and become jealous just like mortals. In the story, they take sides — some of them support the Greeks, while others try to help the Trojans win.

The Greeks

Achilles was the son of the king of the Myrmidons, in Thessaly. His mother was a sea-nymph, or **Nereid**, called Thetis. She told him that his fate was either to win glory and die young or to live a long life without glory. He chose glory and knew when he set off for Troy that he would not return. Achilles was the most handsome and the greatest of the Greek heroes.

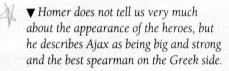

▼ *Homer does not tell us very much about the appearance of the heroes, but he describes Ajax as being big and strong and the best spearman on the Greek side.*

Agamemnon   Diomedes   Achilles   Ajax   Menelaus

Odysseus

8

THE TROJAN WAR

◄ *A golden death mask found by Schliemann in the Mycenaean royal graves. At the time he thought it was the face of King Agamemnon, one of the heroes of the Trojan War. Although this is now thought to be unlikely, it does show the skill of the Mycenaean craft workers.*

Agamemnon was king of Mycenae, and the most powerful prince in Greece. He was the chief commander of the Greeks. He had a lot of authority, although he was not as famous a warrior as Achilles. He was married to Clytemnestra and was Menelaus's brother.

Ajax was the son of Telamon, king of Salamis. He was a huge man, very tall, with broad shoulders, and he was a great warrior.

Diomedes was king of Argos. He was specially protected by the goddess Athena. He was brave as well as wise.

Menelaus was king of Sparta, and Agamemnon's younger brother. He was married to Helen. Menelaus was an athletic-looking man and was intelligent and brave.

Nestor was the king of Pylos. He was a commander during the Trojan War. Because he was too old to fight he acted as a wise counselor to the quarreling Greek leaders.

Odysseus was the son of Laertes, king of Ithaca. He was the smartest of the Greek warriors, as well as being a brave fighter. He was a cunning man, full of tricks, and a very good speaker. He was married to Penelope.

Clytemnestra was the daughter of Leda and Tyndareus, and Helen's half sister. She was married to Agamemnon, but she never forgave him for nearly sacrificing their daughter Iphigenia as an offering to the gods and goddesses on his way to Troy. Clytemnestra later murdered Agamemnon to marry her lover.

Helen was Menelaus's wife, the daughter of Leda and the god Zeus. She was under the power of the goddess Aphrodite, who made her fall in love with the Trojan Paris. Homer shows her as a kind and loving woman who was famous for her beauty.

Penelope was Odysseus's wife. She became queen of Ithaca when Odysseus's father died. While Odysseus was in Troy, Penelope was bothered by dozens of suitors who hoped she would soon be a widow. They wanted to marry her for her palace and her wealth.

The Trojans

The Trojans were also part of the Mycenaean civilization, but their king was Priam, not Agamemnon. The people who supported the Trojans, their **allies**, came from mainland Greece and from Asia Minor.

Aeneas was the son of Anchises and the goddess Aphrodite. He did not fight in the early part of the Trojan War because he had quarreled with Priam. He was called the "soul of the Trojans," and he was a brave and noble fighter.

Antenor was one of the elders of Troy, and the wisest of them.

Hector was King Priam's eldest son and Paris's brother. His mother was Hecuba. He was the chief hero of the Trojans. He felt that Troy was going to fall, but he went on fighting. He preferred death to slavery or disgrace. As well as being a brave warrior, he was a good son, husband, and father.

▶ *The Trojan heroes.*

Aeneas

Hector

The Trojan War

Paris was the second son of Priam and Hecuba. He was a handsome man, fond of women and music. Paris did not wish to fight and was thought of as cowardly.

Priam was king of Troy, and father of Hector, Paris, Cassandra, and many other children. He was married to Hecuba. He was too old to fight in the war.

Andromache was Hector's wife. Her father was king of Thebes, and had been killed by Achilles in a previous war. She knew that Hector was bound to die, and she grieved for him even while he was still alive.

Cassandra was the daughter of Priam and Hecuba, and Hector's sister. Apollo fell in love with her and gave her the gift of seeing into the future, or **prophecy**. Then he punished her, and made sure that no one believed her.

Hecuba was Priam's wife. She had fourteen children, including Hector, Paris, Deiphobos, and Cassandra.

Antenor

Paris

Gods and Goddesses on the Greek Side

Gods and Goddesses on the Greek Side

Athena was the goddess of wisdom and the protector of agriculture, industry, and city defenses. She was the daughter of Zeus.

Hephaestus was the lame god of fire. He was a smith who worked with all kinds of metals. He was the son of Zeus and Hera and was married to Aphrodite.

Hera was the goddess of birth and marriage. She was married to Zeus and often quarreled with him.

Poseidon was the god of the sea, earthquakes, and horses. He lived in the ocean and carried a three-pronged spear, or trident.

Thetis was a sea-nymph and mother of Achilles. She was married to Peleus.

▼ *Athena, the goddess of war, with her helmet and spear.*

▶ *Mount Olympus, the home of the gods.*

THE TROJAN WAR

Gods and Goddesses on the Trojan Side

Aphrodite was the goddess of love and beauty. She was married to Hephaestus but was unfaithful to him with other gods and with Anchises, who was Aeneas's father.

Apollo was the god of music and of prophecy. He also destroyed and punished people for wickedness. He could cause and prevent plague and destruction.

Ares was the god of war. He was hated by the other gods because he was always stirring up conflict. He joined in the fighting out of pure love for war. He was often accompanied by his sister, Eris.

Eris was Ares's sister. She brought misery and strife.

Neutral

Zeus was king of the gods, and all-powerful. He was armed with thunder and lightning.

▲ *Zeus strikes the Greeks with lightning during one of the battles of the Trojan war. Zeus was the god of the sky and controlled the weather, especially storms and thunderbolts.*

13

Why the War Started

E ris, the goddess of strife, was not invited to the wedding of Thetis and Peleus. Furious, she threw a golden apple among the guests. Written on it was, "For the most beautiful."

Hera, Athena, and Aphrodite all claimed the apple. Zeus sent these three goddesses to Mount Ida. Paris was there, and he was asked to judge who was the most beautiful.

Hera promised Paris power and riches, and Athena offered him fame and glory in war. Aphrodite said he could have the most beautiful woman in the world as his wife.

Paris gave the apple to Aphrodite. Shortly after the contest, Paris's father, Priam (the king of Troy), sent Paris as an **ambassador** to Menelaus, the king of Sparta.

Menelaus's wife, Helen, was the most beautiful woman in Greece, almost as beautiful as a goddess. Many men had wanted to marry her, but the god Zeus chose Menelaus for her. Menelaus did not want her disappointed suitors to make trouble — they were all powerful kings and chiefs — so he made them swear an **oath**. If anyone took Helen away from Menelaus, then they would all join forces to get her back.

Aphrodite made Paris fall in love with Helen, and they ran away together. Helen took much of her husband's treasure with her when she left Sparta to sail back to Troy with Paris. Menelaus's brother, Agamemnon, who was king of Mycenae, went to the men who had sworn the oath. He reminded them of their duty, and even wily Odysseus (who did not want to go) had to honor his oath.

The chiefs and heroes gathered at Aulis. They made a sacrifice to the gods and swore that they would bring Helen back to Menelaus. Then they sailed for Troy.

◀ *At the time of the Trojan War, food was stored in pottery jars of various sizes. Archaeologists have found large jars still containing grain and beans. Smaller jars were used for storing oil and wine.*

THE TROJAN WAR

The Fighting Begins

The Trojans knew that the Greeks were coming, and they prepared for a siege. The city walls were repaired and its defenses made stronger. People who lived in outlying villages moved into the city, as they were in danger of raids. Men checked their weapons and everyone stored extra food in their houses.

When the Greeks landed, the Trojans attacked. They killed Protesilaus, who was the first Greek warrior to come ashore, and who had fought bravely. The Trojans were outnumbered, though, and as the Greek soldiers poured from their ships, they forced Hector's warriors back. When Achilles landed and ran to join the fighting, the sight of the famous hero was too much for the Trojans and they quickly retreated into the city.

▼ *The Trojans were on the lookout for the Greeks. As the Greek fleet came into view, Hector led his Trojan warriors down to the shore.*

Peace Talks

The Greeks called a meeting, or **assembly**, and the chiefs agreed that before they fought anymore they should hold peace talks. Odysseus, who was very good at persuading people, agreed to go into Troy with Menelaus. The Trojan Antenor met them at the city gate, called the Scaean Gate, and took them to the palace. Menelaus spoke well and Odysseus was brilliant, but the Trojans were not in a peaceful mood. They wanted revenge for the men who had been killed on the beach as the Greeks landed. They thought the Greeks should have asked for talks first before any fighting started.

Tempers were running high. Odysseus and Menelaus were trapped in an enemy city. They needed to get away quickly, before the Trojans turned on them. Antenor saved them by leading them out of Troy by a back way.

▼ *Antenor meeting Menelaus and Odysseus at the Scaean Gate. He took them through the city to the palace where the peace talks were being held.*

The Trojan War

Since there would be no peace agreement, the Greeks decided to attack the city, but it was too well-defended. The Trojans could not beat the Greeks in open battle, but they could hold Troy.

Stalemate

It was a stalemate. The Greeks realized that they had no hope of taking Troy, with its huge walls and good defenses. The Trojans knew they were safe as long as they did not come out of Troy to fight in the open. So the Greeks turned their attention to attacking the surrounding farms and villages, hoping that the Trojans would come out to protect them. Instead, the remaining country people fled into Troy and helped to defend the city.

Both sides now settled down for a long siege. Homer says that for nine years the Greeks raided the countryside around Troy and up and down the coast. It seemed that the two sides would never come to battle.

▼ *A bronze dagger blade found at Mycenae.*

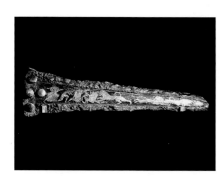

▶ *Weapons and armor that have been found in graves show that the Mycenaean kings and nobles wore armor. Foot soldiers wore leather to protect themselves. Vase paintings also give some clues. The time was still the Bronze Age, and armor and all weapons were made of bronze.*

It seems that body armor was made of bronze plates held together with leather thongs. To protect their heads, warriors wore helmets. There were several styles, depending on which region the warrior came from. Some helmets covered the face, others just covered the head. The helmet could be bronze, and often had horns. The warriors' shields were large and round in shape, and sometimes they used full-length body shields.

The Anger of Achilles

On one of the Greek raids, Achilles captured Chryseis. She was the daughter of the Trojan Chryses, who was a priest of the god Apollo. Agamemnon, as commander in chief of the Greeks, had the pick of any prizes of war, which included captives. Although Achilles had captured Chryseis, Agamemnon decided to keep her as his own servant.

Chryses offered a huge sum of money, a **ransom**, for the return of his daughter. The Greeks wanted to accept the ransom and give Chryseis back, but Agamemnon refused the offer and drove the old priest away.

Apollo Intervenes

Chryses prayed to Apollo to help him against the Greeks. Apollo did; he sent a dreadful illness called a **plague** into the Greek camp. After nine days, Achilles called the Greeks together and held an assembly. He asked Calches to explain why Apollo had sent the plague. Calches was the chief of the **augurs**, people who could understand the meaning of disasters such as plagues. He advised Agamemnon to give Chryseis back to her father.

▲ *Apollo was responsible for the plague that affected the Greek army. It lasted for nine days, killing first the animals and then the soldiers.*

▶ *Achilles was furious with Agamemnon and drew his sword, ready to kill him. Only Athena was able to stop him. She told him to fight with words, not swords.*

THE TROJAN WAR

The Quarrel

Agamemnon insisted that if the Greeks wanted him to give back Chryseis, then they must give him another prize in her place. Achilles objected, saying that Agamemnon could not expect to be given another man's prize. He threatened to leave the war and go back to his home in Phithia. He had no wish to continue winning riches and treasures that Agamemnon took for himself.

Agamemnon told him to go, but said that he was going to take another captive, Briseis, away from Achilles. That would teach Achilles to obey his leader. Briseis was also Achilles's prize, and he loved her. Achilles drew his sword, ready to attack Agamemnon. However, the goddess Athena, unseen by the others, held Achilles back.

Then Achilles turned on Agamemnon, swearing that he would take no more orders from him. He said that one day Agamemnon would need him and his men — the famous Myrmidons — but they would not fight. Achilles went back to his hut, and a messenger arrived from Agamemnon to take Briseis away. When Achilles's mother, Thetis, appeared, he asked her for help, because he wanted to be avenged on Agamemnon.

Agamemnon's Dream

Thetis went to Zeus. He promised to help Achilles, and he made a plan. He called an Evil Dream and told it to go to Agamemnon. While Agamemnon slept, the Dream was to tell him that if he attacked Troy now, the city would fall. Then Zeus would make the Trojans seem to win, and only Achilles would be able to save the Greeks. Agamemnon would have to apologize in order to persuade Achilles to fight.

Homer wrote that after nine years, both sides prepared to fight again. The Trojans came out of their city onto the plain. They were delighted to be going into battle, especially since they thought that Achilles would not be fighting. Achilles was waiting for Zeus to fulfill his promise, and the fighting began again without him.

▲ *Dreams and signs, or **omens**, were important in the ancient world. Agamemnon and the other chiefs believed the Dream sent by Zeus.*

How the War Was Fought

The Greeks and Trojans did not fight like a modern army, with soldiers drawn up in lines or columns. Instead, warriors used spears or fought hand to hand with swords in **single combat**. Homer describes the heroes driving into the front line of battle in their chariots and then fighting on foot. In his day, soldiers did not use chariots. He may not have been sure how people fought in Mycenaean times. Certainly, at the time when the Trojan War took place, people in other cultures did fight from their chariots. This may have happened at Troy, but there is no evidence one way or the other.

Single Combat

The Trojans advanced with yells and shouts. The Greeks marched quickly but silently. The dust of the plain rose high into the air.

When the armies came within fighting distance of each other, they halted. Then a warrior stepped forward from the Trojan lines. It was Paris. He issued a challenge to any Greek soldier to fight him in single combat.

Menelaus was delighted. Here was the cause of all his trouble, ready to fight him. He jumped down from his chariot. Paris saw him, tall and angry in his armor, and immediately he slinked back into the Trojan lines. Hector urged Paris to stand up to Menelaus, and, reluctantly, Paris agreed. Hector shouted to the Greeks to hold their attack.

▼ *Looking like a god, Paris challenged the best of the Greeks to fight him in single combat. Imagine his dismay when Menelaus, Helen's husband, took up his challenge.*

The Trojan War

Paris Escapes

The two sides agreed that Menelaus and Paris should fight in single combat to decide the war. Whoever won would take Helen and her treasure, and there would be friendship between the two armies.

Although Menelaus broke his sword on Paris's helmet, he was the stronger fighter. He grabbed Paris by his helmet and began to drag him back to the Greek lines. But the goddess Aphrodite rescued Paris. She broke the strap holding his helmet and, wrapping him in a thick mist that hid him, carried him off to Helen's room in Troy. Then Hera and Athena made a Trojan archer shoot at Menelaus. This broke the agreement, or **truce**, between the armies. The two sides moved into battle, and the fighting went on all day.

Ajax and Hector

Apollo and Athena finally decided to put an end to the day's fighting. They made Hector challenge a Greek hero to fight him in single combat. At first the Greeks held back, unwilling to take on so great a warrior. Then Ajax came forward to fight. The two heroes fought until night fell. Then they agreed to stop, because neither one was winning. They gave each other gifts and parted as friends.

▼ *Paris, stunned by the blow on his helmet, was swept off his feet by Menelaus and dragged toward the Greek lines.*

Advance and Retreat

The next day, before dawn, the Greeks and Trojans each held a council. The Greeks decided to build a huge mound and extended it with a ditch and walls, or **ramparts**, as a defense for their camps and ships.

Meanwhile, the Trojans urged Paris to give up Helen and the possessions she had brought with her from Sparta. Paris refused to give Helen up but agreed to offer the Greeks her goods. This did not satisfy the Greeks, although they did agree to a day's truce so that both sides could bury their dead.

On the following day, the fighting started again, and this time the Greeks were driven back behind their walls. For the first time the Trojans spent the night out on the plain instead of going back into Troy.

▶ *Odysseus (seated left) pleading with Achilles (seated right) to stop sulking and come and join the war. Standing behind Achilles is his friend Patroclus.*

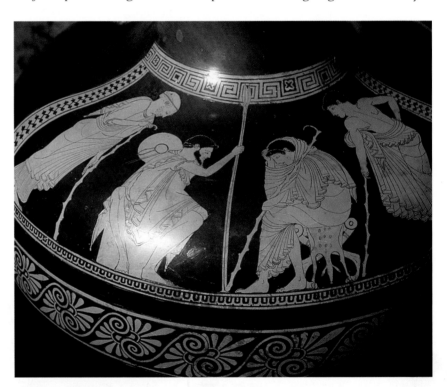

Agamemnon's Offer

Agamemnon really began to be alarmed now. He thought that, after all, the Greeks might not win the war. He suggested that the Greeks pack up and go home, but Nestor advised him to try to persuade Achilles to fight again. Odysseus and Ajax went to Achilles and offered him amazing gifts from Agamemnon. Wealth like this would make Achilles very rich and powerful — and Agamemnon even promised to give Briseis back. Achilles refused the offer.

THE TROJAN WAR

The Next Day

Day dawned. The Greeks plucked up their courage and advanced from their camp. It was a terrible day for them — Agamemnon, Diomedes, and Odysseus were all wounded. The Trojans pressed forward and finally broke through to make a **breach** in the Greek defenses. Only mighty Ajax held the Trojans back.

With Poseidon's help, Ajax stunned Hector with a stone. However, Zeus told Apollo to revive Hector, and once again the Trojans forced the Greeks back — this time as far as their ships. Hector pressed on and began to set fire to the Greek ships.

Patroclus's Plan

Achilles was still waiting. When his greatest friend, Patroclus, failed to persuade him to fight, Patroclus asked if he could borrow Achilles's armor and lead the Myrmidons into battle to try to put out the fires on the Greek ships. Achilles agreed reluctantly, but he warned Patroclus not to try to follow the Trojans as far as Troy. At first the plan worked. Patroclus and the Myrmidons put out the fires and drove the Trojans back across the plain. Then, flushed with success, Patroclus forgot Achilles's advice, and he surged on to Troy itself. As Patroclus was trying to climb, or **scale**, the city walls, the god Apollo hurled him off and knocked his helmet and armor from his body. Unprotected now and dazed, Patroclus was an easy target. Hector killed him with his spear.

▼ *In the midst of the fighting, Ajax tried to defend the Greek ships but was eventually forced back. Some of the Greek ships were set on fire.*

The Death of the Heroes

► *Hephaestus, the blacksmith god. Thetis begged him to make new armor for her son, Achilles, so he could rejoin the fighting.*

Achilles was alone by the ships when he heard that Patroclus was dead. While the Trojans and Greeks fought around Patroclus's body, Achilles mourned for the loss of his friend. Hera roused him, and when the Trojans saw him at the ramparts, shouting defiance at them, they became frightened and fled back to Troy.

Achilles now longed to get back into the fighting, but he could not fight without armor. Thetis begged Hephaestus to make new armor for her son. The lame god worked all night, and by morning Achilles had a magnificent shield, body armor, and helmet. He was ready to fight again.

Achilles went out into battle to find Hector. At first Hector was hidden by the god Apollo, so Achilles slashed his way through the Trojan army looking for him. Aeneas had the courage to stand up to Achilles, but he was no match for him and had to be saved by the god Poseidon.

THE TROJAN WAR

Achilles and Hector

Apollo tricked Achilles and led him away from the battle, which allowed the Trojans to flee back into the citadel. Only Hector stayed outside, waiting by the Scaean Gate. His parents begged him to come into the city, but he would not go. Then, as Achilles approached, Hector lost his nerve and fled. Achilles chased him three times around the walls of Troy. Hector had no chance of winning. Achilles killed Hector with his spear. As Hector died, he told Achilles that he, too, would die soon.

The Poisoned Arrow

Meanwhile, the war went on, with day after day of bloody fighting. Nestor's son was killed, and Achilles, with Odysseus and Ajax, swore vengeance. They chased the Trojans to the Scaean Gate and managed to get inside before the gate was shut. They were inside Troy. Then, as they saw Paris looking down on them, Achilles was struck by a poisoned arrow in his heel. The great hero was dead.

▲ *Before Hector died, he asked Achilles to return his body to Troy for burial. Instead, Achilles tied the dead hero's body to his chariot and dragged it around the walls of Troy. For the next eleven days, Achilles took the body out every day to drag it around his friend Patroclus's tomb. Only when King Priam came and begged for his son's body, offering a ransom for it, did Achilles give it up.*

The Wooden Horse

T he war dragged on. More heroes died. The Greek chiefs met to decide who would have Achilles's armor. Should Odysseus, who stood for wisdom, have it, or Ajax, who was so brave? When the armor was awarded to Odysseus, Ajax became mad with jealousy and finally killed himself. Meanwhile, Paris had died, killed by a poisoned arrow. The Greeks were delighted, but Helen stayed in Troy, now married to Paris's brother Deiphobos.

Odysseus's Plan

The Greeks thought that they would never be able to take Troy by force, so Odysseus made a plan. The Greeks pretended to abandon the siege. Some of the ships sailed away and secretly anchored behind the island of Tenedos. Then the Greeks built a huge wooden horse. It was hollow inside, with room for armed men. The Greeks told the Trojans it was an offering to placate the goddess Athena. They packed up their camp and sailed away in the remaining ships, leaving their huts still smoking.

The Trojans woke to find the Greeks gone. At first, they were suspicious of the wooden horse, but Priam did not want to offend

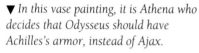
▼ *In this vase painting, it is Athena who decides that Odysseus should have Achilles's armor, instead of Ajax.*

THE TROJAN WAR

◀ *The Trojans pulled the huge wooden horse through the city walls and into the city.*

Athena. He ordered the horse to be dragged across the plain to Troy. It was so big that the Trojans had to break down the city walls to get the horse into Troy — although they rebuilt them again once it was inside. Cassandra shouted that the horse was full of armed men, but no one believed her. Then a priest of Poseidon, named Laocoön, gave a warning. "Never trust Greeks bearing gifts," he said, and threw a spear at the side of the wooden horse. There was a noise from inside, and the Trojans grew alarmed. Now they wanted to burn the horse or throw it over the city walls.

Sinon the Greek

Then a Greek named Sinon arrived. He had been found wandering in the ruins of the camp and had been taken prisoner. He said that he had been badly treated by Odysseus and had escaped to avoid being put to death.

Priam asked him about the wooden horse and Sinon explained that the Greeks had offended Athena — and that was why they had given up the siege. They had made the horse big enough to stop the Trojans from taking it into Troy. Their prophet had told them that if the Trojans could get the horse into Troy, they would win against the Greeks. The mood in Troy changed. As a final proof that Sinon was right and Laocoön wrong, two huge sea serpents came out of the sea and strangled Laocoön and his two sons. Priam then ordered the horse to be taken up to the goddess Athena's **sanctuary** and the citizens of Troy settled down for a night of celebration.

The Fall of Troy

Sinon was not what he had appeared to be. He was Odysseus's cousin and a Greek spy. That night, while everyone in Troy was feasting and celebrating, Sinon went to the walls to light a signal beacon to the Greeks, who were waiting out at sea. Then he let the men out of the horse. Odysseus was guarding the door in the belly of the wooden horse. He led the men out into Troy. Some of them rushed to the gates to let the other Greeks in, and Odysseus and Menelaus ran straight to Helen's house. They killed Deiphobos, and Menelaus was about to kill Helen. Then he looked again at her beauty, and instead of killing her, Menelaus carried Helen away to safety.

▼ While the Trojans were celebrating their victory, Sinon let the Greeks out of the wooden horse while more soldiers waited outside the gate.

The End of Troy

As was usual in war at this time, the invaders killed all the men and boys. They even threw Hector's baby son, Astyanax, to his death from the walls. They dragged the younger women and girls away to the ships, to be taken into slavery.

The Greeks spared Antenor and his family, and the Trojan Aeneas escaped with his son, carrying his aged father on his shoulders. As the fugitives fled, the Greeks were burning their city. After ten long years, the war was finally over. Troy had fallen.

Athena's Anger

Cassandra clung to a statue of the goddess Athena for protection while the city was attacked by the Greeks. The Greeks dragged her away, breaking Athena's statue. This was a terrible offense against the goddess.

THE TROJAN WAR

As a result of Athena's anger, many of the Greeks had difficult voyages home. It took Odysseus ten more years to get back to Ithaca to his wife, Penelope, and his son, Telemachus. Menelaus's ships were swept off course, and he was shipwrecked in Egypt. The two heroes Odysseus and Menelaus survived, but Agamemnon reached Mycenae only to be murdered by his wife, Clytemnestra, and her lover, Aegisthus.

On the Trojan side, Aeneas had his adventures, too. He sailed to Italy and, according to legend, founded Rome. Andromache, Hector's wife, was claimed by Achilles's son, and later she married Helenus, Hector's younger brother, who had also escaped. Cassandra returned to Mycenae with Agamemnon and was also murdered by Clytemnestra.

And beautiful Helen, Helen of Troy as she has been called throughout history? She, of course, lived happily ever after.

▼ *During the sack of Troy, the Greeks threw Astyanax, Hector's baby son, from the ramparts.*

The End of the Story?

The discovery of Troy by archaeologists does not mean that there *was* a war such as Homer describes. The huge city and the vast armies in his poem *The Iliad* are unlikely to have existed in those days. Would a war have been fought over one woman, however beautiful? It seems more likely that Troy interfered with the trade of the other Mycenaean cities, such as Mycenae and Sparta. Troy was a rich city and this would tempt other chiefs to raid it. If, as some experts think, bad harvests had meant that there were fewer goods to trade, the real cause of the war might well have been raids between rival city-states.

Whatever the facts, the story is one of the best-known in the history of Western literature. We may never know whether Helen and Paris, Achilles, Hector, and Odysseus ever existed, but they certainly live on in people's minds. Even today, we still describe a clever trick as "a wooden horse" or say that a brave person "fought like a Trojan."

Glossary

allies: friendly people or countries who agree to fight together against an enemy or to work together for the good of everyone

ambassador: someone who is sent by one country to another country. He or she speaks on behalf of his or her own country to the court, or government, of the other country.

assembly: a meeting of people

augurs: people who knew the meaning of unusual events, such as thunder and lightning. The people in Homer's story believed that events such as these were signs from the gods and goddesses.

breach: a gap in a defensive wall

citadel: a fortified place

immortals: gods and goddesses who cannot die

legend: a well-known tale that may or may not be true. It is usually a tale that has been told for many years, perhaps even hundreds of years.

mortals: ordinary human beings who will die

Nereid: one of the 50 sea-goddesses, or nymphs, who were the daughters of the sea-god Nereus

oath: a promise that a person makes, either to do something or that something he or she has said is true. An oath is usually spoken aloud in the presence of witnesses. To show how seriously the person means to keep the promise, an oath is often made while holding something the person believes to be holy. For example, Christians take oaths while holding the Bible.

omens: happenings that some people believe can tell them about the future. For example, a black cat crossing your path is, to some people, a sign of bad luck to come.

plague: a disease or illness that spreads very quickly and usually kills

plundering: stealing or raiding. Often a raiding party not only stole but also killed people and burned houses.

prophecy: the ability to know what will happen in the future

ramparts: high walls, or banks, that are built for defense. They may be built around a town or as part of a castle.

ransom: a sum of money that is paid to buy back someone who has been taken prisoner

sacrifice: an offering that was given to the goddesses or gods. Oil, wine, animals, and even people were sacrificed to bring a good harvest or good fortune in war.

sanctuary: a place of worship

scale: to climb to the top, for example: of a wall

scholar: a person who studies a subject very carefully and usually for a long time

shrine: a place that is used for religious purposes. It may be a room in a house, part of a church or temple, or even a shelf in a street wall or beside a country lane. There is usually a statue of a god, goddess, or saint, and people leave flowers or other offerings there.

single combat: when two people fight each other, either until one kills the other or until they decide to stop

truce: an agreement to stop fighting

Further Reading

Bowman, John S. *Treasures of Ancient Greece.* New York: Gallery Books, 1986.

Gibson, Michael. *Gods, Men and Monsters from the Greek Myths.* New York: Schocken Books, 1982.

Little, Emily. *The Trojan Horse: How the Greeks Won the War.* New York: Random House, 1988.

Miguel, Pierre. *Life in Ancient Greece.* Morristown, New Jersey: Silver Burdett, 1985.

Payne, Robert. *The Cold of Troy: The Story of Heinrich Schliemann and the Buried Cities of Ancient Greece.* New York: Dorset Press, 1990.

Powell, Anton. *Greece 1600–30 B.C.* New York: Franklin Watts, 1987.

Purdy, Susan Gold and Cass R. Sandak. *Ancient Greece.* New York: Franklin Watts, 1982.

Robinson, Cyril Edward. *Everyday Life in Ancient Greece.* New York: AMS Press, 1977.

Vernant, Jean Pierre. *Myth and Society in Ancient Greece.* New York: Zone Books, 1988.

GREAT BATTLES

Index

PRINTED IN BELGIUM BY
proost
INTERNATIONAL BOOK PRODUCTION